United States Government Accountability Office

Report to Congressional Requesters

I0411869

September 2004

INFORMATION TECHNOLOGY

Major Federal Networks That Support Homeland Security Functions

G A O
Accountability ★ Integrity ★ Reliability

GAO-04-375

INFORMATION TECHNOLOGY

Major Federal Networks That Support Homeland Security Functions

Highlights

Highlights of GAO-04-375, a report to the Chairman, Senate Committee on Governmental Affairs; the Chairman, House Committee on Government Reform, and the Chairman of its Subcommittee on Technology, Information Policy, Intergovernmental Relations and the Census

Why GAO Did This Study

A key information systems challenge in homeland security is ensuring that essential information is shared in a timely and secure manner among disparate parties in federal, state, and local governments, and in the private sectors. This requires communications networks that provide information-sharing capabilities between the various levels of government—federal, state, and local.

GAO's objective was to identify and describe, through agency reporting, major networks and examples of applications that the agencies considered important in supporting their homeland security functions. (For purposes of this review, GAO defined *networks* as "the data communication links that enable computer systems to communicate with each other.") GAO corroborated agency-provided information about networks used by multiple agencies. While agencies verified the accuracy of the data about their networks, GAO cannot ensure that agencies provided data on all applicable networks.

In commenting on a draft of this report, seven of the nine agencies generally concurred with the facts contained in this report. Technical comments were incorporated as appropriate. Two agencies declined to comment.

www.gao.gov/cgi-bin/getrpt?GAO-04-375.

To view the full product, including the scope and methodology, click on the link above. For more information, contact David A. Powner at (202) 512-9286 or pownerd@gao.gov.

What GAO Found

Nine agencies identified 34 major networks that support homeland security functions—32 that are operational and 2 that are being developed (see table). Of these 34, 21 are single-agency networks designed for internal agency communications. Six of the 34 are used to share information with state and local governments; 4 share information with the private sector.

Numbers of Major Federal Homeland Security Networks

	Operational	In development
Unclassified	8	0
Sensitive But Unclassified	17	1
Classified[a]	7[b]	1[c]
	32	2

Source: GAO analysis of agency data.

[a]Excludes classified networks that are not publicly acknowledged.

[b]Secret (5), Top Secret (2).

[c]Secret.

The Department of Homeland Security is in the process of developing the new Homeland Secure Data Network. It is intended to become a significant vehicle for the sharing of homeland security information with state and local governments and classified information among civilian agencies.

Agencies also provided examples of more than 100 major applications that support homeland security mission areas. The following table describes 3 of 18 applications that GAO selected to illustrate the range of applications used to support the various homeland security mission areas.

Three Network Applications That Provide Homeland Security Functions

Mission area	Application	Responsible department	Network
Intelligence and warning	Modernized Intelligence Data Base	Defense	Joint Worldwide Intelligence Communications System[a] (Classified/Top Secret)
Border and transportation security	United States Visitor and Immigrant Status Indicator Technology (US-VISIT)	Homeland Security	Immigration and Customs Enforcement Network (Sensitive But Unclassified)
Domestic counterterrorism	Patriot Act Communications System	Treasury	Treasury Communications System[a] (Sensitive But Unclassified)

Source: GAO analysis of agency data.

[a]Used by other agencies as well.

United States Government Accountability Office

Contents

Abbreviations

APHIS	Animal and Plant Health Inspection Service
CDC	Centers for Disease Control and Prevention
DHS	Department of Homeland Security
DOD	Department of Defense
DOE	Department of Energy
DOJ	Department of Justice
EPA	Environmental Protection Agency
FBI	Federal Bureau of Investigations
FDA	Food and Drug Administration
FEMA	Federal Emergency Management Agency
FSIS	Food Safety Inspection Service
HHS	Department of Health and Human Services
HSDN	Homeland Secure Data Network
HUMINT	human intelligence
IC	intelligence community
JUTNet	Justice United Telecommunications Network
JWICS	Joint Worldwide Intelligence Communications System
LAN	local area network
NIPRNet	Non-Classified Internet Protocol Router Network
OIG	Office of Inspector General
SBU	sensitive but unclassified
SIPRNet	Secret Internet Protocol Router Network
USDA	Department of Agriculture
VPN	virtual private network
WAN	wide area network

G A O
Accountability ★ Integrity ★ Reliability

United States Government Accountability Office
Washington, D.C. 20548

September 17, 2004

The Honorable Susan M. Collins
Chairman, Committee on Governmental Affairs
United States Senate

The Honorable Tom Davis
Chairman, Committee on Government Reform
House of Representatives

The Honorable Adam H. Putnam
Chairman, Subcommittee on Technology, Information
    Policy, Intergovernmental Relations and the Census
House of Representatives

As you know, one of the information systems challenges in the homeland security area is ensuring that critical information is shared in a timely and secure manner with a variety of parties in federal, state, and local governments, as well as in the private sector. It is important that federal networks meet the vital communications needs of effective homeland security, and do so in an efficient manner that includes information sharing between the various levels of government. You asked us to identify the major networks and examples of applications that are operational or being developed by federal agencies to share information in support of homeland security functions.[1]

We conducted work at the federal agencies that have major roles in supporting these homeland security functions and asked agency officials to identify and describe the networks and major applications considered most important in supporting the homeland security functions for which they are responsible. We obtained and analyzed information from 9 agencies on 34 different networks and over 100 applications. We conducted our work from January through July 2004, in accordance with generally accepted government auditing standards.

---

[1]We defined "homeland security" and its related functions according to the Department of Homeland Security's *National Strategy for Homeland Security* (July 2002). It defines homeland security as "a concerted national effort to prevent terrorist attacks within the United States, reduce America's vulnerability to terrorism, and minimize the damage and recover from attacks that occur."

On July 30, we provided your offices with briefing information on the results of this review. The purpose of this letter is to provide the published briefing materials to you. (See app. I.)

In summary, we identified 34 major networks that support homeland security functions—32 operational and 2 in development. Twenty-one of the 34 are single-agency networks, indicating that they are used only for internal agency communications. Further, 6 of the 34 networks share information with state and local governments; 4 share information with the private sector. One of the 2 networks under development—the Department of Homeland Security's (DHS) Homeland Secure Data Network—is intended to become a significant vehicle for future sharing of homeland security information with state and local governments and classified information among civilian agencies. The other network in development, the Department of Justice's JUTNet (Justice United Telecommunications Network), is to replace the department's existing network and transport information among departmental components. Agencies also identified the Internet as a major network for supporting homeland security functions. Cost data were not available for all networks, but of the networks for which data were available, estimates totaled about $1 billion per year for fiscal years 2003 and 2004.

In addition, agencies provided descriptions of over 100 applications as examples of those that use existing networks, including the Internet, to share information in support of homeland security. For example, DHS's United States Visitor and Immigrant Status Indicator Technology (US-VISIT) collects, maintains, and shares information on foreign nationals with the Departments of Commerce, Justice, State, and Transportation using its ICENet (Immigration and Customs Enforcement Network). And, the Department of Defense's Modernized Intelligence Data Base supports anti-terrorist activities through near-real-time, synchronized dissemination of military intelligence using its JWICS (Joint Worldwide Intelligence Communications System) network.

Agency Comments and Our Evaluation

We received written comments on a draft of this report from the Director, Departmental GAO/OIG Liaison at the Department of Homeland Security, the Chief Counsel to the Inspector General at the Department of Health and Human Services (HHS), the Deputy Assistant Secretary and Chief Information Officer at the Department of the Treasury, and the Chief Information Officer at the Department of Agriculture (USDA). These four agencies generally concurred with the facts contained in our report. DHS officials provided technical comments generally consisting of changes to descriptive information, which we incorporated as appropriate. HHS officials provided information on another network it felt should have been included, which we incorporated as appropriate. It also provided additional examples of applications related to homeland security, which we did not include because we had already reported significant examples of applications. The Departments of Defense and Justice, and the Environmental Protection Agency, provided oral comments stating that they concurred with the facts in the report. The Departments of State and Energy declined to comment. Written comments for DHS, HHS, Treasury, and USDA are reproduced in appendices II through V.

Regarding our statement that the initial DHS enterprise architecture does not include many of the networks we identified, DHS stated that the initial enterprise architecture supported internal business processes and systems and that future versions will address federal and other business partners external to DHS. Regarding the Homeland Secure Data Network, the department agreed with our finding that it is a significant initiative for the sharing of classified homeland security information and that it has developed a program plan to allow for future expansion of this effort.

Treasury officials raised concerns regarding the sensitivity of information related to the networks and applications described in this report. We have been cognizant of the sensitivity of this information during the course of this engagement and have asked the agencies to review the report for information they deem too sensitive for public release, which they have done. The information in this report has been approved for public release by the agencies responsible for their specific networks.

As agreed with your offices, unless you publicly announce its contents earlier, we plan no further distribution of this report until 30 days from the date on the report. At that time, we will send copies of the report to the Chairmen and Ranking Minority Members of other Senate and House committees and subcommittees having authorization and oversight responsibilities for homeland security. We will also send copies to the Secretary of Homeland Security and to the other agencies that participated in our review. In addition, the report will be available at no charge on the GAO Web site at http://www.gao.gov.

Should you or your offices have any questions about matters discussed in this report, please contact me at (202) 512-9286 or by e-mail at pownerd@gao.gov. You may also contact M. Yvonne Sanchez, Assistant Director, at (202) 512-6274 or by e-mail at sanchezm@gao.gov. Major contributors to this report also included James C. Houtz, M. Saad Khan, Nicholas H. Marinos, Teresa F. Tucker, and William F. Wadsworth.

David A. Powner
Director, Information Technology Management Issues

Briefing Provided to Staff of Congressional Requesters

Major Federal Networks That Support Homeland Security Functions

Briefing Provided to Staff of Congressional Requesters

July 30, 2004

UPDATED

Table of Contents

2

Introduction
Congressional Requesters

- The Honorable Susan M. Collins, Chairman
  Committee on Governmental Affairs
  U.S. Senate

- The Honorable Tom Davis, Chairman
  Committee on Government Reform
  House of Representatives

- The Honorable Adam H. Putnam, Chairman
  Subcommittee on Technology, Information Policy,
      Intergovernmental Relations and the Census
  Committee on Government Reform
  House of Representatives

3

Introduction

- One of the information systems challenges in the homeland security area is ensuring that critical information is shared in a timely and secure manner to a variety of parties within federal, state, and local governments, as well as in the private sector.

- Ensuring the transmission and receipt of sensitive and in some cases classified information requires communications networks that have adequate security to protect the confidentiality, integrity, and availability of the transmitted information.

- It is important that federal networks meet the vital communications needs for effective homeland security, and do so in an efficient manner that includes productive information sharing among and between the various levels of government.

- We are providing two versions of this briefing, one public and one Limited Official Use Only.

4

Objective, Scope, and Methodology

Objective

To identify major networks and examples of applications that are operated or being developed by federal agencies in support of homeland security functions.

Scope

Conducted work at 9 federal agencies that play major roles in supporting homeland security functions:

- Department of Agriculture (USDA)
- Department of Defense (DOD)
- Department of Energy (DOE)
- Department of Health and Human Services (HHS)
- Department of Homeland Security (DHS)
- Department of Justice (DOJ)
- Department of State
- Department of the Treasury
- Environmental Protection Agency (EPA)

5

Objective, Scope, and Methodology

Methodology

- We asked agency officials to identify and describe the major networks and applications that they considered important in supporting their homeland security functions.

  - We collected descriptive data on the networks, such as type of network topography, primary users, estimated costs, and future plans.

  - We used the homeland security mission areas described in the *National Strategy for Homeland Security*.[1]

- We corroborated the information that agencies provided about networks that are used by multiple agencies.

- Agencies verified the accuracy of the data about their networks; however, we cannot ensure that agencies provided data on all applicable networks.

- We included information about publicly acknowledged classified networks but did not collect or include classified information about these networks.

[1] Published in July 2002.

6

Objective, Scope, and Methodology

Methodology

- We excluded the following types of networks:
    - those used exclusively to support weapons systems and battlefield operations,
    - those that exclusively support radio and other wireless devices, and
    - voice-only networks.
- We conducted our review from January 2004 through July 2004, in accordance with generally accepted government auditing standards.

7

Objective, Scope, and Methodology
Definitions

For purposes of this review, we used the following definitions:

- **Networks** are the data communication links that enable computer systems to communicate with each other.
- **Homeland security**, as defined in the *National Strategy for Homeland Security*, is a concerted national effort to prevent terrorist attacks within the United States, reduce America's vulnerability to terrorism, and minimize the damage and recover from attacks that occur.
- **Top secret** applies to classified information, the unauthorized disclosure of which could reasonably be expected to cause exceptionally grave damage to national security.[2]
- **Secret** applies to classified information, the unauthorized disclosure of which could reasonably be expected to cause serious damage to national security.[2]
- **Sensitive But Unclassified (SBU)** is a generic term used to describe unclassified information that is (1) not required by law to be made available to the public, and (2) sufficiently sensitive to restrict access from public disclosure, but not sensitive enough to warrant a classified designation.[3]

[2]Executive Order 13292: Further Amendment to Executive Order 12958, as Amended, Classified National Security Information (March 25, 2003)
[3]For a historical perspective on SBU, see CRS Report RL31845, *"Sensitive But Unclassified" and Other Federal Security Controls on Scientific and Technical Information: History and Current Controversy* (updated July 2, 2003).

8

Objective, Scope, and Methodology
Data Limitations

- The data presented here do not portray all networks used for information sharing because of the exclusion of classified networks that are not publicly acknowledged.

- The data presented also do not fully portray networks within the intelligence community[4] that support homeland security activities.

---

[4]The intelligence community is comprised of executive branch agencies and organizations that work separately and together to conduct intelligence activities necessary for the conduct of foreign relations and the protection of the national security of the United States.

9

Results in Brief

- Nine agencies identified 34 major networks that support homeland security functions—32 operational and 2 in development.

- DHS has developed an initial version of an enterprise architecture to assist its efforts to integrate and share information among and between federal agencies and other entities; version 1.0 of its architecture does not include many of the networks identified that support these efforts.

- Cost information was not available for some networks—of the cost information that was available for fiscal years 2003 and 2004, the cost estimates totaled about $1 billion per year.

- DHS's Homeland Secure Data Network appears to be a significant initiative for future sharing of classified homeland security information among civilian agencies and DOD.

- Agencies identified over 100 examples of major applications that support the homeland security missions areas; we selected 18 examples to illustrate the range of applications that are used across federal agencies.

- The Internet has also been identified as a major network for supporting homeland security applications.

10

Background
Department of Homeland Security

- On November 25, 2002, the Homeland Security Act of 2002 (Public Law 107-296) established the Department of Homeland Security (DHS).

- DHS is required to coordinate efforts across all levels of government and throughout the nation, including federal, state, tribal, local, and private-sector homeland security resources.

- DHS's mission is accomplished by various departmental components that are responsible for, among other things,

    - enforcing immigration and customs laws and providing effective border and transportation system defense against external threats;

    - preparing for, mitigating the effects of, responding to, and recovering from all domestic disasters, including acts of terror; and

    - providing intelligence analysis of terrorist threat information and mitigating the vulnerabilities in the nation's critical infrastructure.

11

Background
Department of Homeland Security

- According to the President's *National Strategy for Homeland Security*, part of DHS's responsibilities is to coordinate and facilitate the sharing of information both among its component agencies and with other federal agencies, state and local governments, the private sector, and other entities.

- In August 2003, we reported that DHS had begun to develop an enterprise architecture and that it planned to use this architecture to assist its efforts to integrate and share information among federal agencies and between federal agencies, state and city governments, and the private sector.[5]

[5]GAO, *Homeland Security: Efforts to Improve Information Sharing Need to Be Strengthened*, GAO-03-760 (Washington, D.C.: Aug. 27, 2003).

12

Background
Previously Reported DHS Management Challenges

- As reported in GAO's 2003 high-risk series:[6]
  - DHS faced challenges to improving IT management during the transformation to the new department.
    - Future needs must be sufficiently identified in order for DHS to build effective systems that can support the national homeland security strategy.
    - DHS inherited IT problems from several of the agencies being incorporated into the new department.
  - The government's ability to leverage information sharing between and among important government and private sector stakeholders must be strengthened.
- We noted the importance of addressing these challenges in order for DHS and other federal agencies to maximize the use of existing networks and to plan for the successful implementation of new networks.

[6]GAO, *Major Management Challenges and Program Risks: Department of Homeland Security*, GAO-03-102 (Washington, D.C.: January 2003).

13

Background
Other Federal Agencies' Roles in Supporting Homeland Security Functions

Department of Defense (DOD)

- Carry out military missions abroad that reduce the terrorist threat to the United States.

- Protect United States territory, domestic populations, and critical infrastructure against military attacks emanating from outside the United States, under the operation of the Northern Command.[7]

- Support civil authorities under emergency circumstances when asked to act quickly and provide capabilities that other agencies do not have or for limited scope missions where other agencies have the lead (also called "military assistance to civil authorities" or "civil support").

Department of State

- Develop, coordinate, and implement counterterrorism policy and building international coalitions to identify and eliminate terrorist networks.

- Review and process applications for visas to visit the United States and denying visas to applicants who pose a danger to national security.

[7]Also known as homeland defense.

14

Background
Other Federal Agencies' Roles in Supporting Homeland Security Functions

Department of Justice (DOJ)

- Prevent terrorist acts before they occur, and investigate and prosecute those who have committed or intend to commit these acts.
- Combat espionage by strengthening counterintelligence capabilities.

Department of Health and Human Services (HHS)

- Provide critical expertise and resources related to bioterrorism.
- Coordinate the deployment of medical personnel, equipment, and pharmaceuticals among federal agencies and the American Red Cross in cases of terrorist attacks when medical consequences exceed local and state capabilities.
- Provide health warning information.

15

Background
Other Federal Agencies' Roles in Supporting Homeland Security Functions

Department of the Treasury

- Develop and implement federal strategies to combat terrorist financing domestically and internationally.

- Participate in the development and implementation of federal policies and regulations in support of the USA PATRIOT Act.

Department of Energy (DOE)

- Safeguard and secure nuclear weapons complexes and stored stockpile material.

- Provide technology, analysis, and expertise to aid federal agencies in preventing the spread or use of weapons of mass destruction (i.e., radiological, chemical, and biological).

16

Background
Other Federal Agencies' Roles in Supporting Homeland Security Functions

Department of Agriculture (USDA)

- Protect the nation's agriculture sector and the meat and poultry areas of the food sector from terrorist attacks.

Environmental Protection Agency (EPA)

- Secure the nation's drinking and wastewater infrastructure, the chemical industry, and the hazardous materials sector.

- Minimize the impact to indoor and outdoor air from terrorist attack.

- Respond to and recover from acts of biological, chemical, certain radiological, and other terrorist attacks.

17

Background
Description of Networks

- The term *network* refers to the data communication links and the network elements such as routers and switches that enable these computer systems to communicate with each other.

- A network in a small geographical area is known as a local area network (LAN); most organizations have one or more LANs at each of their offices.

- Wide area networks (WANs) connect multiple LANs within an organization that is dispersed over a wide geographical area.

- The term *network* also refers to virtual private networks (VPN) which are communication systems that use public networks to securely transport private intra- and interorganizational information.

18

Background
Example of a Typical Network

Computer systems are interconnected into LANs and WANs and are often connected to the Internet

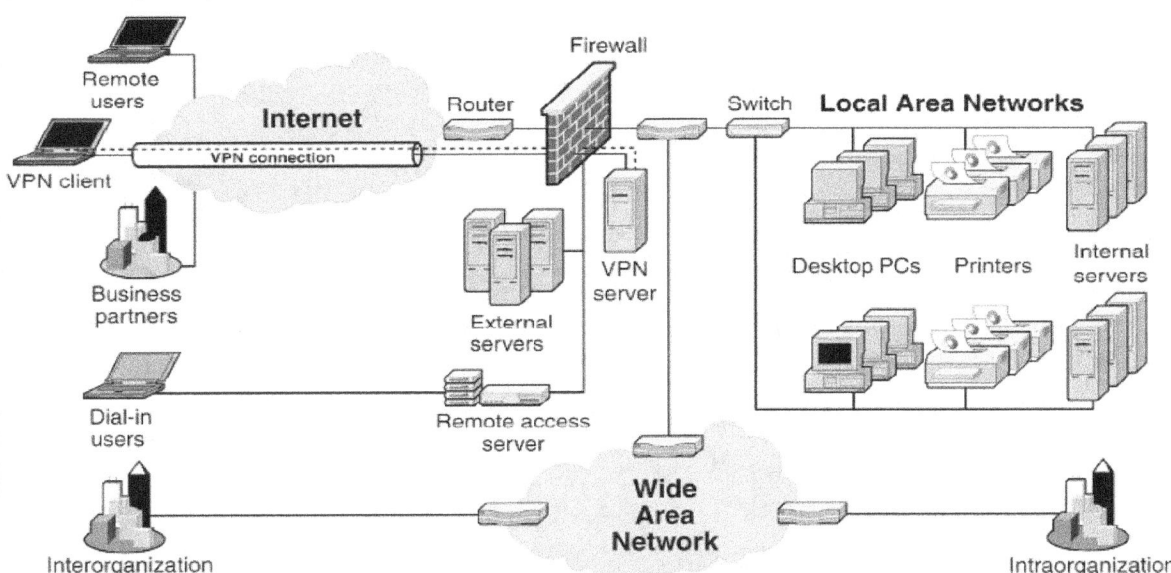

Sources: GAO analysis and Microsoft Visio.

19

Background

Use of Networks for Homeland Security

According to the *National Strategy for Homeland Security:*

- Information sharing and information systems contribute to every aspect of homeland security, but our country's information systems have not adequately supported the homeland security mission.

  - The *National Strategy* aligns homeland security functions into 6 critical mission areas, as described on page 32.

- Two fundamental problems have prevented the federal government from building efficient governmentwide information systems.

  - Government acquisition of information systems has not been coordinated and agencies have not pursued compatibility across the federal government or with state and local entities.

  - Cultural barriers often prevent agencies from exchanging and integrating information.

20

Major Homeland Security Networks
Overview on the Use of Networks in Federal Agencies

- Agencies identified 34 networks that are used to support homeland security

    - 8 publicly acknowledged classified networks—7 operational and 1 in development;

    - 18 sensitive but unclassified (SBU) networks—17 operational and 1 in development; and

    - 8 unclassified operational networks.

- 21 of 34 are single-agency networks; these are internal networks that support individual agencies' missions by transmitting information within each agency (e.g., connections between field and headquarters offices, access to internal information systems, and agency-level communications).

21

Major Homeland Security Networks
Overview on the Use of Networks in Federal Agencies

- DHS has developed an initial version of an enterprise architecture to assist its efforts to integrate and share information among and between federal agencies and other entities; version 1.0 of its architecture does not include many of the networks identified that support these efforts.

- Six networks are used to share SBU and unclassified information with state and local governments; 4 share information with the private sector.

- Cost information was not available for some networks often due to the inability to separate network-specific cost information from overall program budget, as well as cost information deemed classified or sensitive by the agency.

  - For the cost information that was available, for fiscal years 2003 and 2004, the cost estimates totaled just over $1 billion per year.

22

Major Homeland Security Networks
Classified Networks[8]

- Classified networks are used primarily to share intelligence and law enforcement information within and between federal agencies.
- 5 federal agencies manage and maintain 8 publicly acknowledged classified networks in use today—7 operational and 1 in development.
    - There are 2 operational top secret networks.[9]
    - There are 5 operational secret networks.
    - There is 1 secret network in development.

[8]Classified networks are described in appendix I.
[9]These networks are also classified as sensitive compartmented information, which is classified information derived from intelligence services, methods, or analytical processes; such information is handled by procedures established by the Director of Central Intelligence.

23

Major Homeland Security Networks
Classified Networks

Top Secret Networks		Primary Network Users								
		DOD	DHS	DOJ	State	Treasury	USDA	DOE	Other Fed	IC[a]
Existing	Joint Worldwide Intelligence Communications System (JWICS)	❖	◆	◆	◆	◆		◆	◆	◆
Existing	Sensitive Compartmented Information Operational Network			❖						
Secret Networks		DOD	DHS	DOJ	State	Treasury	USDA	DOE	Other Fed	IC[a]
Existing	ClassNet				❖					
Existing	Emergency Communications Network/ Classified							❖		
Existing	Federal Bureau of Investigation Network			❖						
Existing	HUMINT Operational Communications Network	❖								◆
Existing	Secret Internet Protocol Router Network (SIPRNet)	❖	◆	◆	◆	◆	◆	◆	◆	◆
In Dev	Homeland Secure Data Network		❖							

❖ Agency responsible for managing and using the network
◆ Agency that uses the network
[a] Intelligence community

Source: GAO analysis of agency data.

24

Major Homeland Security Networks
Classified Networks

- DHS is in the process of developing the new **Homeland Secure Data Network**, which is expected to
  - provide services for transmitting secret information for DHS and civilian agencies that currently rely on DOD's SIPRNet;
  - eventually be able to carry all types of data up to secret and may eventually support the transmission of top secret information;
  - provide classified e-mail and Web sites, messaging, data analysis tools, collaboration tools, and other applications required to support DHS; and
  - connect to other classified networks, including SIPRNet.
- According to DHS, fiscal year 2004 expected cost is $20 million; the lifecycle cost has not yet been determined.

25

Major Homeland Security Networks
Classified Networks

Homeland Secure Data Network (continued):

- The Homeland Secure Data Network appears to be a significant initiative for sharing classified information among civilian agencies.
- Phase 1 is to be deployed during the first quarter of fiscal year 2005.
  - Includes access to about 125 high-priority sites—about 70 DHS sites and over 50 state and local sites, including the transition of DHS officials from SIPRNet.
- Phase 2 is to be deployed during the second quarter of fiscal year 2005.
  - Includes continued deployment to other DHS and state and local sites.
- Phase 3 is to be deployed during the third quarter of fiscal year 2005.
  - Includes connection to other federal civilian agencies.
- As of July 2004, DHS was in the early stages of planning and had not yet coordinated with other agencies to determine their technical requirements for classified network services or overall transition plans from SIPRNet to the Homeland Secure Data Network.

26

Major Homeland Security Networks
Sensitive But Unclassified Networks[10]

- 5 agencies manage 18 networks that share SBU information internally, among federal agencies, with state and local governments, and with the private sector—17 operational and 1 in development.

    - 11 networks share information only within an agency.

    - 2 networks share information only with other federal agencies.

    - 5 networks share information with state and local government agencies or the private sector.

- DHS has completed work to connect its multiple, disparate SBU and unclassified legacy networks through the DHS Core Network, although some DHS users are still in a transition phase and are operating on their previous agencies' networks.

[10]SBU networks are described in appendix II.

27

Major Homeland Security Networks

Sensitive But Unclassified Networks

	SBU Networks	Primary Network Users											
		DOD	DHS	DOJ	State	Treasury	USDA	HHS	DOE	EPA	Other Federal	State/ Local	Private Sector
Existing	Air National Guard Enterprise Network[a]	❖											
Existing	Army Reserve Network	❖											
Existing	Coast Guard Data Network Plus	◆	❖								◆	◆	◆
Existing	Corp of Engineer Enterprise Infrastructure Services	❖											
Existing	Criminal Justice Information Services WAN	◆	◆	❖	◆			◆		◆		◆	
Existing	Critical Infrastructure Warning Information Network	◆	❖	◆	◆						◆	◆	◆
Existing	Customs and Border Protection Network		❖			◆					◆	◆	
Existing	DHS Core Network		❖										
Existing	FEMA WAN		❖										

❖ Agency responsible for managing and using the network
◆ Agency that uses the network

Source: GAO analysis of agency data
[a] Also supports some classified information

28

Major Homeland Security Networks
Sensitive But Unclassified Networks

SBU Networks		Primary Network Users											
		DOD	DHS	DOJ	State	Treasury	USDA	HHS	DOE	EPA	Other Federal	State/ Local	Private Sector
Existing	GuardNet	❖											
	ICENet		❖	◆	◆		◆				◆	◆	◆
	Justice Consolidated Network			❖									
	Medical TRICARE Network	❖											
	Non-Classified IP Router Network (NIPRNet)	❖	◆								◆		
	OpenNet				❖								
	Secret Service WAN		❖										
	Treasury Communications System		◆	◆		❖							
In Dev	Justice Unified Telecommunications Network			❖									

❖ Agency responsible for managing and using the network
◆ Agency that uses the network

Source: GAO analysis of agency data.

29

Major Homeland Security Networks
Sensitive But Unclassified Networks

- DOJ is in the process of implementing the **Justice Unified Telecommunications Network**, which is expected to
  - increase the agency's existing capability to share information by replacing its existing SBU network,
  - carry all types of data (e.g., videoconferencing and voice over Internet protocol services), including classified data, and
  - transmit information relating to the investigation and prosecution of crimes and terrorist activities among DOJ's components.
- Implementation is planned for the end of 2004.
- According to DOJ, fiscal year 2003 costs are $3 million and the estimated fiscal year 2004 costs are $4 million.
- While final decisions have not been made, connectivity is being planned to allow information sharing with DHS or other government agencies.

30

Major Homeland Security Networks
Unclassified Networks[11]

5 agencies manage 8 networks that share unclassified information within an agency, between federal agencies, with state and local governments, and with the private sector.

Unclassified Networks	Primary Network Users											
	DOD	DHS	DOJ	State	Treasury	USDA	HHS	DOE	EPA	Other Federal	State/ Local	Private Sector
Animal and Plant Health Inspection Service Enterprise WAN		◆				❖						◆
Centers for Disease Control and Prevention Network							❖				◆	
Diplomatic Telecommunications Service	◆	◆	◆	❖	◆	◆				◆		
DOE Corporate Network								❖				
Emergency Communications Network/ Unclassified								❖				
EPA WAN									❖			
Food and Drug Administration WAN							❖					
Food Safety Inspection Service WAN						❖						

Existing

❖ Agency responsible for managing and using the network
◆ Agency that uses the network

[11]Unclassified networks are described in appendix III.
Source: GAO analysis of agency data.

31

Homeland Security Applications
Homeland Security Mission Areas

Intelligence and warning	To detect terrorist activity before it manifests itself in an attack so that proper preemptive, preventive, and protective action can be taken.
Border and transportation security	To promote the efficient and reliable flow of people, goods, and services across borders, while preventing terrorists from using transportation conveyances or systems to deliver implements of destruction.
Domestic counterterrorism	To identify, halt, and where appropriate, prosecute terrorists in the United States, pursuing not only the individuals directly involved in terrorist activity but also their sources of support.
Protecting critical infrastructure and key assets[12]	To improve protection of the individual pieces and interconnecting systems that make up our critical infrastructure, making us more secure from terrorist attacks and reducing our vulnerability to natural disasters, organized crime, and computer hackers.
Defending against catastrophic threats	To prevent terrorist use of nuclear weapons, detect chemical and biological materials and attacks, improve chemical sensors and decontamination techniques, and develop vaccines and antidotes.
Emergency preparedness and response	To minimize the damage and recover from future terrorist attacks that may occur by bringing together and coordinating all necessary response assets quickly and effectively.

[12]This mission area aligns closely with the other areas and is therefore represented by all of the application examples.

32

Homeland Security Applications
Overview

- Agencies identified over 100 examples of major applications that support the various homeland security missions areas; we selected 18 examples that illustrate the range of applications that are used across the government:
  - 4 examples that support intelligence and warning,
  - 3 examples that support border and transportation security,
  - 5 examples that support domestic counterterrorism,
  - 2 examples that support defending against catastrophic threats, and
  - 4 examples that support emergency preparedness and response.
- Agencies at times used the term *network* to describe computer systems or applications that communicate with each other through the use of data communications links; for purposes of this review, we categorized these as *applications.*
- Federal agencies are increasingly relying on the Internet to provide information-sharing services with other federal agencies, with state and local governments, and with the private sector.

33

Homeland Security Applications
Use of the Internet

Agencies identified the Internet as a major public network for supporting homeland security functions. For example:

- DHS is using the Internet through the Homeland Security Information Network, a collection of systems that support two-way communications of SBU information among DHS, governors' offices, homeland security advisers, and the National Guard.

- DOD has established a virtual private network via the Internet for the SBU Anti-Drug Network, a drug-interdiction community made up of federal agencies, the intelligence community, law enforcement officials, and private enterprises.

- DOJ has established an Internet-based network, the Regional Information Sharing System Network, for exchanging criminal intelligence with law enforcement officials and first responders.

- HHS is using digital certificates for secure information exchange over the Internet to support the Public Health Information Network.

34

Homeland Security Applications
Examples That Support
Intelligence and Warning

- DOD's **Modernized Intelligence Data Base** is reported to provide near-real-time and synchronized dissemination of military intelligence in support of antiterrorist activities.

  - Uses DOD's JWICS to interface with intelligence and war fighter databases and applications

- The State Department's **Consular Lookout and Support System** is reported to provide information about individuals who were refused a visa or passport and those who are considered a potential national security threat.

  - Uses State's OpenNet network to provide information to consular officers involved in the visa issuance process, passport agencies, other federal agencies, and the international community

35

Homeland Security Applications
Examples That Support
Intelligence and Warning

- DHS's **Pathfinder** is a search tool that was developed to store all Coast Guard intelligence message traffic and intelligence reports.
  - Uses DOD's SIPRNet to provide information to intelligence analysts.
- DOJ has supported the implementation of the **Regional Information Sharing System Network**, which is a communications network administered by state and local law enforcement to exchange SBU criminal intelligence among law enforcement officials, including information on potential threats.
  - Uses the Internet to provide information to law enforcement and first responder communities
  - DOJ has several new pilot projects with DHS, DOD, State, and other entities to expand information sharing among federal, state, and local law enforcement and other entities.

36

Homeland Security Applications
Examples That Support
Border and Transportation Security

- DHS's **Treasury Enforcement Communications System** is reported to provide support for passenger processing and investigations.
  - Uses the Treasury Communications System network to provide (1) border inspection, investigative, interdiction, intelligence analysis, and integrity tracking support software, and (2) communications to federal, state, and international law enforcement

- DHS's **United States Visitor and Immigrant Status Indicator Technology** is to collect, maintain, and share information on foreign nationals.
  - Uses ICENet to provide information to the Departments of Commerce, Homeland Security, Justice, State, and Transportation

- DHS's **Automated Targeting System** is reported to electronically review and prioritize data for exports, imports, and airline passengers to identify cargo and passengers most likely to threaten national security.
  - Uses the Internet to provide information to Customs and Border officials

37

Homeland Security Applications
Examples That Support
Domestic Counterterrorism

- Treasury's **PATRIOT Act Communications System** is reported to be a secure messaging system that communicates and disseminates information such as advisories and reports on the latest trends in money laundering or terrorist financing.
  - Uses the department's network to provide information to its Financial Crimes Enforcement Network and financial institutions
- DOD sponsors the **Anti-Drug Network**, a community that was established to support drug-interdiction activities.
  - Uses an Internet-based virtual private network to provide unclassified information to DOD officials, diplomats, the intelligence community, law enforcement, private enterprises dealing with governments, and state, local, and foreign governments
  - Uses SIPRNet to provide classified information to DOD officials, diplomats, the intelligence community, law enforcement, the Federal Communications Commission, and the Executive Office of the President

38

Homeland Security Applications
Examples That Support
Domestic Counterterrorism

- DOJ's **Integrated Automated Fingerprint Information System** is reported to identify individuals from submitted fingerprints and provide records on criminals, including terrorists.
  - Uses the Criminal Justice Information Services WAN to provide criminal history information to federal, state and local agencies as well as other authorized licensing and employment agencies.
- DOJ's **National Crime Information Center** system is reported to provide information on individuals, vehicles, or property associated with terrorist organizations or crimes.
  - Uses the Criminal Justice Information Services WAN to provide information to all law enforcement agencies and officers, including federal, state, and local officials
- DOJ's **Law Enforcement Online** is a data repository that was developed to store SBU data and provide a hub for the law enforcement community and other related networks.
  - Uses a secure Internet-based virtual private network to provide information for federal, state, and local law enforcement agencies

39

Homeland Security Applications
Examples That Support
Defending Against Catastrophic Threats

- DOD's **Joint Biological Point Detection System** is to detect, identify, sample, collect, and communicate the presence of biological warfare agents in order to enhance the survivability of United States forces.

  - Consists of complementary trigger, sampler, detector, and identification technologies that allow it to rapidly and automatically detect and identify biological threat agents

- DHS's **BioWatch**—a combined effort with HHS and EPA using environmental sensors in over 30 cities around the country—is reported to monitor the air for potential biothreat agents. The system uses filter pads that collect air samples that are tested for the presence of any agents.

  - Some information is currently disseminated across federal agencies by voice communications, although efforts are under way to use the Internet to share data.

  - Laboratory test results are shared electronically with HHS.

40

Homeland Security Applications
Examples That Support
Emergency Preparedness and Response

- DHS's **National Emergency Management Information System** is reported to provide automation support for core emergency management functions, including emergency coordination efforts and disaster assistance for individual victims.

  - Uses the FEMA Network to provide information to federal, state and local response operations, and for support of public assistance and mitigation programs for state and local government recovery efforts

- DHS's **Homeland Security Information Network** was implemented to provide a collaborative two-way tool that supports federal, state, and local law enforcement and intelligence programs by providing connectivity to government agencies

  - Uses the Internet to provide situational awareness, decision support, and event reporting, as well as support for national special security events.[13]

[13]When an event is designated by DHS as a *national special security event*, federal resources are deployed to maintain security, with the Secret Service as the lead federal agency for implementation of the operational security plan.

41

Homeland Security Applications
Examples That Support
Emergency Preparedness and Response

- HHS's **Public Health Information Network** is reported to support public health activities, including bioterrorism preparedness and response, by deploying and coordinating systems across the health care community.

  - Uses the Internet to provide event detection, outbreak management, lab result reporting, disease surveillance, health alerts, and knowledge management information to the public health community—local and state health departments, HHS, and other federal agencies

- DHS's **Disaster Management Interoperability Services** is reported to provide the capability for the emergency management community to share digital information across geographically dispersed entities.

  - Uses the Internet to provide automated tools for responding to an incident by alerting first responders, graphically displaying incidents on a national map, and exchanging tactical information

42

Summary

- Nine agencies identified 34 major federal networks that support homeland security functions.

  - Approximately two-thirds of the networks identified are single-agency networks that only share information internally.

- DHS has developed an initial version of an enterprise architecture to assist its efforts to integrate and share information among and between federal agencies and other entities; version 1.0 of its architecture does not include many of the networks identified that support these efforts.

- Cost information was not available for some networks often due to the inability to separate network-specific cost information from overall program budget—of the cost information that was available for fiscal years 2003 and 2004, the cost estimates totaled about $1 billion per year.

43

Summary

- DHS's Homeland Secure Data Network appears to be a significant initiative for future sharing of classified homeland security information among civilian agencies, although still in the early planning stages.

    - Questions remain about coordination with other government agencies to determine their technical requirements for classified network services and overall transition plans from DOD's SIPRNet to the Homeland Secure Data Network.

- Agencies provided examples of applications that are used across the federal government, which illustrate the range of applications that support homeland security missions areas.

    - The Internet has also been identified as a major network for supporting homeland security applications.

44

Agency Comments

- We received oral comments on a draft of these briefing slides from all 9 federal agencies
- Agency officials agreed with the facts presented and provided technical comments, which we incorporated in this document as appropriate.

45

Appendix I
Description of Classified Networks

Responsible Agency	Network Name	Network Description
DHS	Homeland Secure Data Network (HSDN) (planned)	HSDN will transport classified homeland security data in support of activities including intelligence, investigations, and inspections. HSDN will serve as the replacement for SIPRNET's secret connectivity for civilian agencies.
DOD	HUMINT Operational Communications Network (HOCNet)	HOCNET is used for the dissemination of secret-level human intelligence (HUMINT) information in support of the Defense HUMINT Service.
	Secret Internet Protocol Router Network (SIPRNet)	SIPRNet is a global WAN used to transmit secret data in support of homeland security activities, including drug interdiction operations and anti-terrorist activities, such as customs and border patrol operations and law enforcement activities.
	Joint Worldwide Intelligence Communications System (JWICS)	JWICS is a global WAN used for the dissemination of top secret military intelligence information-- voice, video, and data--in support of anti-terrorist activities
DOE	Emergency Communications Network/Classified (ECN/C)	ECN/C provides encrypted exchange of real-time emergency event information between DOE's National Nuclear Security Administration field offices, the national laboratories, and headquarters.
DOJ	Federal Bureau of Investigations Network (FBINet)	FBINet is used for communicating secret information, including investigative case file and intelligence pertaining to national security.
	Sensitive Compartmented Information Operational Network (SCION)	SCION is a global WAN that transports secret and top secret data. It is less than 2 years old and will support applications now being developed related to aid counterterrorism efforts.
State	Class Net	ClassNet is a global WAN that transports classified and unclassified data in support of State Department activities, including secure messaging between State executives and U.S. diplomats, and access to classified web sites.

Source: GAO analysis of agency data.

46

Appendix II
Description of Sensitive But Unclassified Networks

Responsible Agency	Network Name	Network Description
DHS	Coast Guard Data Network Plus (CGDN+)	CGDN+ is used to transmit data such as maritime-related law enforcement information and intelligence supporting drug interdiction, border control, and emergency sealift management.
	Critical Infrastructure Warning Information Network (CWIN)	CWIN is a secure network for voice and data used to transmit data on infrastructure protection, communication and coordination, alert, and notification. In the event a significant attack disrupts the telecommunications networks or the Internet, CWIN provides secure capability for communications across key government network operations centers (NOC), as well as private sector and trusted foreign partner NOCs.
	Customs and Border Protection Network	The CBP Network is used to transmit SBU data related to CBP's support of homeland security functions, such as protecting the nation's borders from terrorists, and regulating and facilitating the lawful movement of goods and persons across U.S. borders.
	DHS Core Network (DCN)	DCN is used to transmit SBU data related to DHS' directorates' homeland security functions, such as customs and border patrol, intelligence and warning, and counter-terrorism.
	Federal Emergency Management Agency (FEMA) WAN	FEMA WAN provides support for emergency coordination of federal, state, and local operations, disaster assistance, and government recovery efforts.
	Immigration and Customs Enforcement Network (ICENet)	ICENet provides data to support immigration enforcement at points of entry and application service centers, and provides data to support border patrol, anti-smuggling units, and air operations.
	Secret Service WAN	The Secret Service WAN transports SBU data used to support protective services for the President and to investigate financial crimes.
DOJ	Criminal Justice Information Services (CJIS) WAN	CJIS WAN provides data entered by state, local, tribal, and federal law enforcement agencies on individuals, vehicles, and property associated with crimes or terrorist organizations. It is also used to identify individuals from submitted fingerprints and to exchange DNA information.
	Justice Consolidated Network (JCN)	JCN is used to transmit data relating to the investigation and prosecution of crimes and terrorist activities among DOJ components.
	Justice Unified Telecommunications Network (JUTNet) (planned)	JUTNet is a planned network that will be used to transmit classified and unclassified information relating to the investigation and prosecution of crimes and terrorist activities.

Source: GAO analysis of agency data.

47

Appendix II
Description of Sensitive But Unclassified Networks

Responsible Agency	Network Name	Network Description
DOD	Air National Guard Enterprise Network	Air National Guard Enterprise Network provides emergency response information--voice, video, and data--to Air National Guard state missions and civil emergency response teams that respond to civil and natural disasters. It also provides local connection to NIPRNet and SIPRNet.
	Army Reserve Network (ARNet)	ARNet WAN transports information--voice, video, and data-- for planning and supporting Army Reserve homeland defense and homeland security activities.
	Corp of Engineers Enterprise Infrastructure Services (CEEIS) WAN	CEEIS WAN transports information--voice, video, and data--related to water and flood control, civil works, navigation, and power generation.
	GuardNet	GuardNet is an operational infrastructure that provides connectivity between National Guard components and the Army. It transports information--voice, video, and data--for planning and supporting National Guard homeland defense and homeland security activities. GuardNet can, at the direction of DOD, be extended to the state and local level for their use.
	Medical Command (MEDCOM) Tricare Network	MEDCOM Tricare Network provides information--voice, video, and data--to support the medical command throughout the wartime theater of operations as well as peace operations, humanitarian assistance and operations in aid of civil authorities.
	Non-classified Internet Protocol Router Network (NIPRNet)	NIPRNet is a global WAN used to transmit unclassified data within DOD and with other select federal agencies.
State	Open Net	OpenNet is a global WAN that transports unclassified data in support of the foreign and domestic activities of the State Department, including information for processing visa and passport applications.
Treasury	Treasury Communications System (TCS)	TCS' network services are used to transport data related to combating terrorist financing. It also transmits information to support the homeland security activities of several law enforcement agencies that transitioned either to DHS or DOJ.

Source: GAO analysis of agency data.

48

Appendix III
Description of Unclassified Networks

Responsible Agency	Network Name	Network Description
DOE	DOE Corporate Network (DOEnet)	DOEnet is the agency's core network infrastructure that transports data in support of DOE's corporate activities and links headquarters to select field offices.
DOE	Emergency Communications Network/Unclassified (ECN/U)	ECN/U transports unclassified information--voice, video, and data--providing secure exchange of real-time emergency event information between DOE's National Nuclear Security Administration field offices and headquarters.
EPA	EPA Wide Area Network	The EPA WAN is the agency's national network that connects headquarters, regions, laboratories and field offices. It transports unclassified information that supports EPA's homeland security activities, including the protection of drinking water and air quality, and recovery from biological, chemical, and certain radiological terrorist attacks.
HHS	Centers for Disease Control and Prevention Network (CDCNet)	CDCNet is a WAN that links all its major facilities. It transports unclassified data in support of CDC's homeland security activities including infectious diseases surveillance, outbreak management, and countermeasures management.
HHS	Food and Drug Administration (FDA) WAN	The FDA WAN is the agency's network that links all its major facilities. It transports unclassified data in support of FDA's homeland security activities in support of import approval, health warning information alerts, biologics marketing approval, and post-market drug and biologics health warning regulatory communications.
State	Diplomatic Telecommunications System (DTS)	DTS is a global telecommunications service that provides WAN connectivity for all federal agencies at overseas diplomatic and consular posts. It supports various customer interfaces (e.g., serial, IP, ATM) over diverse transmission paths such as terrestrial, satellite and Internet VPNs. DTS is funded by a mix of direct appropriations and reimbursements from customer agencies.
USDA	Animal and Plant Health Inspection Service Enterprise (APHIS) WAN	APHIS WAN provides data on plant and animal products including associated health certificates and the tracking of product movements.
USDA	Food Safety Inspection Service (FSIS) WAN	FSIS WAN provides data used to select food items to be inspected. It also provides information on the results of laboratory tests, and helps analyze consumer complaints in order to identify contaminants in the food supply, including possible intentional acts.

Source: GAO analysis of agency data.

49

Comments from the Department of Agriculture

United States
Department of
Agriculture

Office of the Chief
Information Officer

1400 Independence
Avenue S.W.

Washington, DC
20250

August 25, 2004

David A. Powner, Director
Information Technology Management Issues
General Accounting Office

Dear Mr. Powner:

The United States Department of Agriculture (USDA) has reviewed draft report number GAO-04-375 entitled "INFORMATION TECHNOLOGY: Major Federal Networks That Support Homeland Security Functions" and is in agreement with the facts as they relate to USDA.

Thank you for the opportunity to review and comment on the draft report. If additional information is needed, please contact Marilyn Holland of my staff on (202) 720-6275.

Sincerely,

Scott Charbo
Chief Information Officer

Comments from the Department of the Treasury

Comment: We acknowledged
neither locations nor paths of
specific programs; rather we
only provided general
descriptions of the networks
identified.

DEPARTMENT OF THE TREASURY
WASHINGTON, D.C. 20220

SEP 2 2004

Mr. David A. Powner
Director
Information Technology Management Issues
General Accounting Office
441 G Street, NW, Room 5T37
Washington, DC 20548

Dear David:

Thank you for the opportunity to review and to comment on your draft report entitled
"Information Technology" Major Federal Networks That Support Homeland Security Functions"
(Report #GAO-04-375). I concur with the GAO's findings and its assessment.

In reviewing the document, however, I have a concern over acknowledging the location and path
used for the Department of Homeland Security (DHS) specific programs. Publicly documenting,
in one document, where major DHS applications are operated and how they are connected may
present a significant physical and electronic risk and cause them to become more significant
targets.

The major Treasury contributor to DHS support is the Treasury Communications System (TCS).
TCS's network services are used to transport data related to combating terrorist financial. It also
transports information to support the homeland security activities of several law enforcement
agencies that transitioned either to DHS or the Department of Justice. It is also the medium of
transport for the DHS's Treasury Enforcement Communications System, and the Treasury's
PATROIT Act Communications System (Financial Crimes Enforcement Network). The
Treasury TCS network is a secure enterprise network providing Treasury secure Internet,
Intranet and e-mail services and continues to provide these services to both Treasury and other
federal agencies. We are proud of the diverse, redundant, secure, and survivable TCS that we
have improved on since 9-11.

Finally, I want to underscore my commitment to supporting the Homeland security functions of
Treasury and that of DHS.

If you have any questions regarding our comments, please contact me at 202-622-1200 or via
email at ira.hobbs@do.treas.gov

Sincerely,

for Ira L. Hobbs
Deputy Assistant Secretary and
Chief Information Officer

Comments from the Department of Homeland Security

U.S. Department of Homeland Security
Washington, DC 20528

Homeland
Security

September 8, 2004

Mr. David A. Powner
Director, Information Technology Management Issues
General Accounting Office
Washington, DC 20548

Dear Mr. Powner:

Re: Draft Report GAO-04-375, Information Technology, Major Federal Networks
that Support Homeland Security Functions (GAO Job Code 310459)

Thank you for the opportunity to review the findings referenced in the draft report. In the
review of federal networks, GAO highlighted that the initial Department of Homeland
Security (DHS) Enterprise Architecture (EA) does not include many of the networks
external to DHS that support information sharing between federal agencies and other
entities. When the Department was formed in March of 2003, we began our initial efforts
around EA. Version 1.0 of the DHS EA was developed in approximately four months
from essentially a "clean sheet of paper." The focus of the initial DHS EA was to
primarily support transformation of internal DHS business processes and systems.
Subsequent versions of our EA will increasingly address federal and other partners
external to DHS essential to support the homeland security mission. Version 2.0 of our
EA is scheduled for release this fall.

Additionally, the report noted that the DHS Homeland Secure Data Network (HSDN)
could serve as a significant initiative for sharing of classified homeland security
information among civilian agencies. The Department is in agreement with your
findings; and to that end has developed the HSDN program plan to allow for the
expansion of the network to any federal agency with a need to share classified homeland
security information. DHS has begun preliminary discussions with a significant number
of federal agencies on the possibility of meeting their technical requirements for
classified network services. Administration policy on this topic, allocation of resources,
and schedules to meet agreed to requirements are still in the formative stage.

www.dhs.gov

The Department anticipates increased clarity and firm plans for other federal agency participation in HSDN to be completed over the next six months. Per our discussion, this assumes incorporation of our technical comments which were provided to you under separate cover.

We thank you again for the opportunity to provide comments on the findings in this report.

Sincerely,

Anna F. Dixon
Director, Departmental GAO/OIG Liaison
Office of the Chief Financial Officer

Comments from the Department of Health and Human Services

DEPARTMENT OF HEALTH & HUMAN SERVICES Office of Inspector General

Washington, D.C. 20201

SEP   2 2004

David A. Powner
Director, Information Technology
    Management Issues
United States Government Accountability Office
Washington, D.C. 20548

Dear Mr. Powner:

Enclosed are the Department's comments on your draft report entitled, "Information Technology: Major Federal Networks That Support Homeland Security Functions" (GAO-04-375). The comments represent the tentative position of the Department and are subject to reevaluation when the final version of this report is received.

The Department provided several technical comments directly to your staff.

The Department appreciates the opportunity to comment on this draft report before its publication.

Sincerely,

Lewis Morris
Chief Counsel to the Inspector General

Enclosure

> The Office of Inspector General (OIG) is transmitting the Department's response to this draft report in our capacity as the Department's designated focal point and coordinator for Government Accountability Office reports. OIG has not conducted an independent assessment of these comments and therefore expresses no opinion on them.

COMMENTS OF THE DEPARTMENT OF HEALTH AND HUMAN SERVICES (HHS) ON THE GOVERNMENT ACCOUNTABILITY OFFICE'S (GAO) DRAFT REPORT "INFORMATION TECHNOLOGY: MAJOR FEDERAL NETWORKS THAT SUPPORT HOMELAND SECURITY FUNCTIONS" (GAO-04-375)

HHS appreciates the opportunity to review the GAO draft report.

HHS's Food and Drug Administration (FDA) has several networks that support homeland security functions which were not included in the report. FDA maintains four assets in its Critical Infrastructure Protection (CIP) inventory: (1) Regulatory Management System (RMS); (2) FDA Operational and Administrative System Import Support (OASIS); (3) CFSAN Adverse Event Reporting System (CAERS); and (4) CDER Adverse Event Reporting System (AERS). These assets were identified in a collaborative process with FDA, HHS, and the Department of Homeland Security (DHS). In fact, DHS viewed these assets as the top four for all of HHS.

Each of these assets runs over the FDA network, much like that of the Centers for Disease Control and Prevention (CDC). In fact, a description of the "FDA Wide Area Network" would be essentially identical to CDC's (page 49 of the report), except for mention of FDA's specific homeland security functions in support of import approval, health warning information alerts, biologics marketing approval, and post-market drug and biologics health warning regulatory communications.

GAO Comment

Agencies identified over 100 examples of major applications that support the homeland security missions areas; we selected 18 examples to illustrate the range of applications that are used across Federal agencies.

HHS Response

The report did not specifically list the "examples of more than 100 major applications" (page 10, bullet 5); therefore, it is not clear that the systems identified below were included in the GAO assessment/inventory.

- Field Accomplishments and Compliance Tracking System (FACTS) – Automated FDA system for tracking FDA operations such as domestic field and compliance activities, foreign inspections, and domestic and import sample analyses.

- Food Firm Registration Module (FFRM) – FDA system which requires domestic and foreign facilities that manufacture/process, pack, or hold food for human or animal consumption to register their facility under Section 305 of the Public Health Security and Bioterrorism Preparedness and Response Act of 2002.

1

Registration is one of several tools which will enable FDA to act quickly in responding to a threatened or actual terrorist attack on the U.S. food supply by giving FDA information about these facilities. In the event of an outbreak of foodborne illness, such information will help FDA and other authorities determine the source and cause of the event, and in the future may enable FDA to quickly notify the facilities that might be affected by the outbreak.

- Prior Notice System Interface (PNSI) and the Automated Broker Interface of the Automated Commercial System (ABI/ACS) – Import shipment information submitted to FDA that allows information pertaining to FDA-regulated shipments of food for humans and animals be reviewed in advance of the food being imported into the U.S. (unless the food is excluded from Prior Notice requirements of Section 307 of the Bioterrorism Act of 2002).

- The Electronic Laboratory Exchange Network (eLEXNET) – A seamless, integrated, secure system that allows multiple government agencies engaged in food safety activities to compare, communicate, and coordinate laboratory analysis findings. This network provides the necessary infrastructure for an early-warning system that identifies potentially hazardous foods and enables health officials to assess risks and analyze trends. This network is funded by FDA and supported by the U.S. Department of Agriculture and the Department of Defense.

- Food Emergency Response Network (FERN) – Cooperative expansion of eLEXNET system to encompass a nationwide network of Federal and State laboratories capable of analyzing foods for agents of concern.

- FDA Emergency Operations Network (EON) - EON, with the Incident Management System (IMS) as its cornerstone, provides a central hub for exchanging and relaying emergency-related information among FDA offices and external stakeholders. EON IMS brings together individual commercial off-the-shelf software (COTS) solutions supporting incident tracking, contact management, collaboration and knowledge tool management, Geographic Information System (GIS), and email into an integrated web-based application to facilitate the management and organization of the large volume of incident information. The system is cited specifically in FDA's annual performance plan in support of the agency's counter-terrorism goals and is developed in accordance with HSPD-5, "Management of Domestic Incidents" and establishment of a National IMS.

2

GAO's Mission	The Government Accountability Office, the audit, evaluation and investigative arm of Congress, exists to support Congress in meeting its constitutional responsibilities and to help improve the performance and accountability of the federal government for the American people. GAO examines the use of public funds; evaluates federal programs and policies; and provides analyses, recommendations, and other assistance to help Congress make informed oversight, policy, and funding decisions. GAO's commitment to good government is reflected in its core values of accountability, integrity, and reliability.
Obtaining Copies of GAO Reports and Testimony	The fastest and easiest way to obtain copies of GAO documents at no cost is through GAO's Web site (www.gao.gov). Each weekday, GAO posts newly released reports, testimony, and correspondence on its Web site. To have GAO e-mail you a list of newly posted products every afternoon, go to www.gao.gov and select "Subscribe to Updates."
Order by Mail or Phone	The first copy of each printed report is free. Additional copies are $2 each. A check or money order should be made out to the Superintendent of Documents. GAO also accepts VISA and Mastercard. Orders for 100 or more copies mailed to a single address are discounted 25 percent. Orders should be sent to:

U.S. Government Accountability Office
441 G Street NW, Room LM
Washington, D.C. 20548

To order by Phone: Voice: (202) 512-6000
TDD: (202) 512-2537
Fax: (202) 512-6061

To Report Fraud, Waste, and Abuse in Federal Programs	Contact: Web site: www.gao.gov/fraudnet/fraudnet.htm E-mail: fraudnet@gao.gov Automated answering system: (800) 424-5454 or (202) 512-7470
Congressional Relations	Gloria Jarmon, Managing Director, JarmonG@gao.gov (202) 512-4400 U.S. Government Accountability Office, 441 G Street NW, Room 7125 Washington, D.C. 20548
Public Affairs	Jeff Nelligan, Managing Director, NelliganJ@gao.gov (202) 512-4800 U.S. Government Accountability Office, 441 G Street NW, Room 7149 Washington, D.C. 20548